GW00733458

This is a fictionalised biography describing some
of the key moments (so far!) in the career of
Heung-min Son.
Some of the events described in this book are
based upon the author's imagination and are
probably not entirely accurate representations
of what actually happened.

Tales from the Pitch
Heung-min Son
by Harry Coninx

Published by Raven Books
An imprint of Ransom Publishing Ltd.
Unit 7, Brocklands Farm, West Meon, Hampshire GU32 1JN, UK
www.ransom.co.uk

ISBN   978 180047 121 4
First published in 2021

Copyright © 2021 Ransom Publishing Ltd.
Text copyright © 2021 Ransom Publishing Ltd.
Cover illustration by Ben Farr © 2021 Ben Farr

A CIP catalogue record of this book is available from the British Library.

All rights reserved. No part of this publication may be reproduced, stored in a
retrieval system, or transmitted, in any form or by any means, electronic, mechanical,
photocopying, recording or otherwise, without the prior permission of the
publishers.

The rights of Harry Coninx to be identified as the author and of Ben Farr to be
identified as the illustrator of this Work have been asserted by them in accordance
with sections 77 and 78 of the Copyright, Design and Patents Act 1988.

TALES FROM THE PITCH

HEUNG-MIN SON

HARRY CONINX

RAVEN

For Tunde, to get you interested in football again

CONTENTS

I
FOUR

September 2020, St Mary's Stadium, Southampton, England
Southampton v Tottenham

Son turned away as Danny Ings went through on goal and put Southampton 1-0 up.

It was only the second game of the new season, but already Son was beginning to fear the worst. Spurs had lost their opening game 1-0 to Everton and now they were trailing here. It certainly didn't feel like the start of a title-winning season.

"Come on, Sonny!" Ben Davies shouted, kicking the ball back up to the half-way line. "We need you! Let's get going!"

Son nodded grimly and took a deep breath. He needed to wake up and get involved. There was still an hour left – plenty of time for Spurs to get themselves back in the game.

"Sonny, push up," Harry Kane shouted to him. "They're playing a high line and you'll get space in behind. Let me drop deep and I'll play it through for you."

Son shrugged and swapped places with Kane, moving higher up the pitch. He'd played as a striker plenty of times before, but that was usually when Kane was injured. Now he was up alongside him. Son trusted Harry to know what he was doing, so he was happy to follow his advice.

With seconds to go before half-time, Spurs got their chance.

Tanguy Ndombele played the ball out wide to Kane on the left-hand side and with his first touch Kane fizzed the ball towards the box.

Kane didn't even need to say anything – Son was already on the move.

Son saw the keeper coming out and braced himself for a challenge. But the keeper suddenly stopped and started backtracking. But Son knew he was going to get there first.

With his first touch he got the ball out from under his feet and out of reach of the surrounding defenders. With his second touch he blasted it past the keeper and into the far corner of the goal.

GOAL! Spurs were level.

"I told you, mate," Kane said as they celebrated. "There's chances for you here! They just can't handle your pace!"

Despite the goal, manager José Mourinho was furious at half-time.

"We're too slow," he raged. "They're quicker than us and they're stronger than us. Do you guys want to win this match? Because I need winners out there."

The dressing room was silent. A few players looked at the floor, nodding quietly.

"Sonny, that goal was brilliant," José said, turning

towards Son. "We need more like that, OK? Harry is right – let him drop deep and you play up there. You *will* get goals today."

Son looked up at his manager. It still felt surreal at times like this that he was being spoken to by José Mourinho, one of the greatest managers of all time – and now *his* manager.

He would never get used to that.

Two minutes into the second half, Son got his next chance.

Again it was Kane who poked the ball into his path. Son was level with a Southampton defender and they both chased after the ball. The defender was stronger, but Son was quicker.

He nipped ahead of the defender, knocking the ball forward with his right foot. As the keeper came out, Son lashed it past him with his left foot.

GOAL!

Spurs had turned the game on its head. They were now 2-1 up.

"I suppose you'll want me to set you up for a hat-trick now," Kane laughed.

Kane might have been joking, but 15 minutes later that's exactly what happened.

Kane dropped deep and collected the ball just inside the Spurs half. Son was already running – he didn't even need to worry about where Kane was.

Seconds later, the ball was at his feet. Then suddenly it was in the back of the net.

GOAL!

It wasn't the first hat-trick of Son's career, but this one felt particularly sweet. All the disappointments about Spurs' start to the season were beginning to disappear.

"I thought you were supposed to set *me* up," Kane said, as he joined the celebrations.

"Are you guys going to let anyone else have a go?" Erik Lamela asked with a grin.

Son laughed, but he knew they still had 25 minutes of the game left to play. 3-1 was a good scoreline, but they could do even better. He wanted more goals.

Ten minutes later he got his wish. Kane got the ball on the right and whipped in a cross towards Son. He controlled the ball with his chest and then dinked it past the keeper.

GOAL!

Son had four! He didn't even know if there was a word for getting four in a game. And all four goals had been assisted by Harry Kane. He didn't think anything like that had ever happened before.

"As long as you two keep playing like this, I think we should do pretty well this year," Lamela laughed, as Son celebrated the goal.

Lamela was right. With Spurs eventually winning the game 5-2, Son now knew that, as long as Spurs had him and Kane, they could beat anyone.

This might finally be the year he lifted a trophy for his club.

2
KEEPIE-UP

August 2002, Son's childhood home, Chuncheon, South Korea

"It's your turn to go in goal!" Son shouted, glaring across the garden at his brother. The sun was fierce and he felt a bead of sweat trickle down his forehead.

"No way!" his brother, Heung-yun, replied, staring back at him. "I've just been in goal – now it's your turn!"

"But I'm a striker," Son protested. "I'm going to be shooting way more in games than you ever will."

"I'm *not* going in goal and that's that," his brother hissed. "I'm older, so it's my turn to shoot."

"Wait, wait," Son said. "How about a keepie-uppie competition? Loser has to go in goal."

Heung-yun thought for a moment. "OK," he said. "Let's do it."

"Great," Son replied. "But – new deal," he added. "The person who loses has to go in goal for the rest of the day."

"Fine."

Son grabbed a second ball from the far corner of the garden and they both set themselves up.

"First person to drop the ball loses," Son said. "Three … two … one … GO!"

They both started confidently, but after a while Son realised that this could go on for a while. Both brothers had the skills just to keep on going.

There was only one option for Son now. He kicked his ball higher and then, just before it hit the ground, he swung at it, volleying it towards Heung-yun. The ball struck his brother, who instantly lost control and both balls bounced away on the ground.

"Your ball hit the ground first!" Son said. "I win!"

"No way! You cheated!" his brother protested. "You kicked the ball at me!"

Suddenly Heung-yun charged at Son, and the two boys fell to the floor, wrestling and pushing at each other.

"Oi!"

The shout came from behind them. It was their dad, Son Woong-jung, who'd come out to see what all the noise was about.

"What's going on?" he asked sternly, as the boys picked themselves up, still glaring at each other.

"We were trying to decide who goes in goal," Heung-yun explained, "and we were doing a keepie-uppie competition ... "

" ... and your little brother cheated as usual, did he?" their dad continued.

Their dad always knew exactly what was going on. He'd been a footballer when he was younger, although he hadn't made it at the highest level. Now he was a coach for their local football team and he had a reputation for his discipline and tough training routines.

But Son Woong-jung always saved his highest expectations for his two sons. They might not have realised it yet, but every punishment and every demand he made of them was designed to make them better footballers.

He wanted them to succeed where he hadn't.

"Well, if you love keepie-uppies so much," he continued, "then you can stay out here for the next four hours, each keeping your ball in the air."

They both stared at him, open-mouthed.

"And if you drop it, then you can start again from the beginning." He kicked the two balls towards them and walked back into the house.

"I'll be watching," he shouted over his shoulder, "so don't drop it."

The brothers knew their father well enough to know that he was completely serious.

So, keeping a fair distance apart, both boys began. This time they were both completely focused on keeping the ball in the air.

Hours later, Son let the ball drop and saw his brother do the same.

He didn't know if they'd been out in the garden for four hours, but he was glad his dad had finally come out to tell them they could stop.

There was a sly smile on their dad's face as he let them back into the house. It hadn't *quite* been four hours, but he hadn't actually expected either of them to last as long as they had.

It was clear to him that his coaching was working well. Both boys were well on their way to making it as footballers.

"Maybe there's hope for you two after all," he chuckled to himself as he let them into the house.

3
SPONGEBOB

August 2006, Son's childhood home, Chuncheon, South Korea

"Why are we watching this?" Heung-yun shouted to his fourteen-year-old brother, wrenching the remote out of his hands.

"Hey!" Son replied, snatching it back before his brother could change the channel. "It's funny! I like it!"

"It's not in Korean," his brother said, gesturing at the TV. "It's not even in English! What's the point?"

"It's in German," Son said quietly.

"What?!" his brother shouted, dumbstruck. "Why are you watching Spongebob Squarepants in German? That's *so* stupid! What's wrong with you?"

"It's useful!" Son replied. "Do you know how many Asian players got their big break in Germany? How else am I going to learn the language?"

"OK. Name one player who got a break in Germany," his brother said. "Go on … I'm waiting."

Son looked at the floor, trying to think of just one name to give to Heung-yun.

"Cha bum-kun, for a start," came a firm voice from behind them. Once again, their dad had snuck up behind the pair and caught them in the middle of an argument.

"Exactly!" Son said, glad his dad had taken his side and come up with a name.

Cha bum-kun wasn't just any old player either – he was one of South Korea's greatest ever players, and he'd got his big break in the Bundesliga.

"Just because you watch Spongebob in German doesn't mean you're going to be as good as him,"

Heung-yun scoffed, rolling his eyes at Son and poking his tongue out behind their dad's back.

"Don't laugh," their dad said. "Your brother's doing the right thing. If you want to make it to the top, you're going to need to play in Europe at some point – and you'll need a couple of languages under your belt."

He gave his sons a steely glare.

"After all, how many of the world's top managers speak Korean?"

4

FIRST GAME

August 2006, GS Champions Park, Guri, South Korea

Son sat in the changing room and laced up his boots, hardly able to contain his excitement at finally getting to play in a proper football match.

For a long time his dad Son Woong-jung had refused to let the two boys play in real matches on full-sized 11-a-side pitches.

He'd been very clear. He said matches on full-sized

pitches were just too hard for younger players and would do more harm than good – to their bodies *and* to their developing football skills.

As always, the boys were happy to go along with his advice. They knew that, in the long term, it would help their football.

Even so, now that the big day had come, Son couldn't wait. He changed quickly and before long he was out warming up on the pitch.

"Focus on your touches and your passing today," his dad said. "I don't want any crazy dribbling or shooting, unless you're in the perfect position."

Son nodded. He knew how his dad liked the game to be played.

He started out on the right wing and it took a few minutes before he got his first touch. It was a poor one and he lost the ball.

But he recovered quickly and darted after the ball, beating the closest opposition player. Flicking the ball round the defender, Son was away. He raced down the wing, the ball at his feet, as he sized up the next defender.

"Release it!" his dad roared. "Pass it now!"

Son checked his run, then slipped a pass back to a team-mate.

"Well done!" his dad shouted encouragingly.

Son continued to play well and in the second half he found himself playing on the same side of the pitch as his dad. He could hear his dad constantly in his ear, telling him where to go, when to pass the ball, where to position himself …

It was a continuous running commentary.

Well into the second half, Son finally got his chance. A firm tackle from one of his team-mates saw the ball come out towards him. The opposition striker went down, but the ref waved for play to go on.

Son took the ball and saw clear space in front of him. He could hear his dad shouting, but there was only one thing he had in his mind now. He sprinted forward, bearing down on the defenders with the ball at his feet.

The first defender tried to tackle him, but the challenge was poor and Son rounded it easily. The second defender stumbled and Son skipped past him, leaving him on the floor.

Now it was just him and the keeper.

Son pretended to shoot with his right foot and the keeper committed himself, diving to the floor.

Then Son nipped the ball onto his left foot and strolled around the keeper. A moment later, he tapped it in.

GOAL!

"Come on!" Son shouted, as a few of his team-mates ran over to him to celebrate. It was his first 'real' goal – in his first 'real' game.

Son looked across to the touchline, but he could only see a scowl on his dad's face. Son thought that was probably because he'd dribbled the ball and then taken a shot, instead of passing it to a team-mate as his dad would have wished.

Standing behind their dad, Heung-yun gave Son a big smile and a thumbs-up.

Before the other team could get the game started again, his dad made a couple of subs, pulling Son off too.

It was a friendly match, so Son just assumed that his dad was giving a few of the other players a chance to play.

"Why did you ignore me?" his dad demanded as soon as Son was off the pitch.

"What? I didn't hear you," Son replied.

"Did you see the player down, injured?" his dad continued, gesturing to the opposition striker, who was still down.

"Yeah, but it wasn't a foul," Son said. "And the ref said 'play on'."

"I don't care about the ref," his dad continued, "and I don't care that you scored. If a player is injured, you put the ball out. It doesn't matter how good you are at football – if you can't respect the other players then you're nobody. You understand?"

Son nodded and took a seat next to the rest of the players. He felt deflated.

He knew that his father was right – and he knew in his head that he was doing the best for him. But being told off like this still wasn't pleasant. The good feelings he'd had before the game and after scoring had now completely gone.

Heung-yun came over and sat down next to his brother.

"Don't worry about him," he said. "It was a great goal."

"Thanks," Son answered, obviously disappointed at his dad's reaction.

"And guess who I've seen over there," his brother continued. "Scouts. From some of the biggest clubs in Europe, people were saying."

"What?" Son gasped in surprise.

"Yeah," his brother said with a grin. "There's scouts from Germany and England and everything. And someone said they're only here to look at one player. *You*."

"Wow." Son cheered up almost immediately.

A whirlwind of different thoughts started to race through his mind. He could already picture himself playing in the Bundesliga, scoring the winning goal in a critical game … then winning the cup …

"Maybe watching Spongebob in German wasn't so crazy after all," joked his brother.

5

A TASTE OF HAMBURG

August 2008, Hamburg Youth Academy, Hamburg, Germany

"Hey Sonny," Markus, the Hamburg youth coach, shouted to him as they finished the training session. "Come with me!" He gestured for Son to follow him, leading him back onto the pitch.

The rest of the players were trudging over to the dressing room. The rain had just started to come down and they were all looking forward to getting indoors.

"You don't mind a bit of rain, do you?" Markus chuckled.

"This?" Son laughed. "This is nothing."

"Right answer," Markus laughed. "OK, let's have a go at this then."

Heung-yun had been right. There *had* been scouts from Germany at the matches in Korea and, soon afterwards, Son and two other South Korean players had joined Hamburg in the Bundesliga, as part of a Korean federation exchange programme.

He would only be with the German club for a month or two, before going back to Korea at the end of the exchange, but for Son, still only 16, it was the biggest opportunity of his life so far.

His dad had insisted on making the trip to Germany with him. "You'll need me there," Son Woong-jung had said. "We'll do some extra training in the evenings, make sure you're miles ahead of the other lads there."

Son had been nervous about such a big move, having to deal with a new country, a new language and, of course, a new top-level club.

It helped a lot to have a few other South Koreans

with him. Even though he'd been working on his German, getting himself well past the Spongebob stage, Son's language skills still weren't good enough to get by with a team full of German players.

One thing that he was finding easier, though, was the football. He'd worried that he might not be fit enough, but he was pleasantly surprised by how easily he adapted to his opening weeks in the Hamburg set-up.

There were no huge, six-foot-five-inch centre-backs to knock him over, and the ball was played at pretty much the same pace as it was back in Chuncheon.

As it turned out, Son wasn't just adapting to German football – he was smashing it.

So the additional training sessions with Markus at the club were a welcome opportunity to learn more about the German game and to hone his skills.

As the rain intensified, Markus laid out a row of cones leading up to the penalty area. Then he pointed to the goal, where there was a bag hanging over each corner, strapped to the crossbar.

"OK, Sonny. Dribble through the cones and then shoot to hit the bag," Markus explained.

"Wouldn't it make more sense to aim for the bottom corner?" Son asked. "I'd never aim that high in a proper match."

"This isn't about a proper match," Markus replied. "It's about accuracy and technique. I want you to hit the bags."

Son grabbed a ball and got himself into position. He dribbled past the first cone, then controlled the ball around the others. As soon as he got to the end of the cones, he heard the shout from Markus.

"Shoot now, Sonny!"

He whipped the ball with his right foot, aiming for the bag in the top-left corner. The ball banged off the crossbar and flew behind the goal.

"Nope," Markus replied. "Try again."

For the next hour, Son continued dribbling between the cones and then shooting, aiming at each corner in turn. He was forced to shoot with his right foot, then his left.

"You need to train both feet," Markus told Son. "There isn't a single good player who's one-footed – it's pointless."

Son was exhausted by the end of it, and to make matters worse he'd only hit the bags a couple of times.

At the end of the session he was expecting harsh words from Markus. He felt as if he might as well have gone in with the rest of the team at the end of training. This had obviously been a waste of time.

"Well done, kid," Markus said, slapping him on the back as they finished. "Come on, let's get inside."

"Sorry, I barely hit the bags," Son said quietly. "I know I can do better."

"You did great," Markus laughed. "I'd have been shocked if you'd hit them every time. In sessions like this we don't ask you to do stuff you can already do. That's why it's called training."

Despite his disappointment, Son was buzzing as he walked back into the dressing room. He was having his first taste of what life might be like in the Bundesliga, training and developing his skills with a top German club.

Now he was absolutely sure – he *had* to play in the Bundesliga. Somehow, he had to make it happen.

6
BUNDESLIGA

November 2009, Hamburg Youth Academy, Hamburg,
Germany

"Hey Sonny!" Markus shouted, a huge smile on his face. "Come on! Over here!"

Son jogged slowly over to Markus, part of him hoping it wasn't an extra drill. He knew these extra sessions were really developing his skills, but they were exhausting, especially alongside his training sessions with the rest of the players.

"You're training with the first team today," Markus grinned. "They're a man short."

"What?" Son said, surprise showing on his face.

"Yep – just for today," Markus replied. "Go on! Get over there, show them what you're made of!"

It was now a year after Son's first exchange programme trip to Hamburg. He'd had to go back to South Korea after that initial visit, but he'd already known, even then, that he'd be returning to join Hamburg permanently for the following season.

The other two South Koreans he'd come over with initially hadn't been so lucky – they hadn't been selected, so were now back in Korea. That had been a gentle reminder of how hard he needed to work, and how lucky he was to be here.

Coming back to Hamburg had changed his dad's attitude too. Son Woong-jung had never been too focused on Son's shooting and dribbling skills, thinking it was more important for his son to learn how to play more of a team role on the pitch.

But now he realised that, as Son developed into a striker, shooting was going to be an important part of his son's game. As a result, father and son were now spending half their extra training sessions practising shooting. To Son, it felt as if his dad was finally supporting him in becoming the player he really wanted to be.

During the summer, Son had also made his international debut for South Korea in the U-17 World Cup. It had been his first taste of international football and, although South Korea had been knocked out before the final, it had been one of the best experiences of his career so far.

"Next time we're going to win one," he'd told his dad excitedly. "I can't wait!"

"Let's focus on getting you in the Hamburg team first," his dad had warned him. "Sometimes it's better to prioritise your club career at this early stage."

So now, with Markus nodding in the direction of the training pitch, Son jogged over to join the first team for their training session.

As he rounded the corner he stopped, suddenly feeling starstruck. Directly in front of him were all the famous names who made up the Hamburg team.

There was Zé Roberto, the legendary Brazilian defender, Jérôme Boateng, Mladen Petric´ and, most impressive of all, Ruud van Nistelrooy.

The Hamburg first-team manager, Bruno Labbadia, waved Son over.

"You're up front with Ruud," he said, pointing at the pitch, where the game had already started. He didn't bother with any introductions, instead just pushing Son onto the pitch.

Son was nervous as he approached Ruud. The man was a legend who'd scored hundreds of goals for Real Madrid and Man United, and had won countless trophies.

Now they were training together.

But before he could even compose himself, Son saw Ruud gesturing for him to come over and join him on the pitch.

"You're with me, kid," Ruud said simply. "You do the running and I'll find you," he added.

Son nodded, eager to impress his experienced team-mate.

The game went by quickly – much too quickly for

Son's liking. He hadn't got a lot of the ball and everyone had clearly been a level above him – a bit stronger, a bit faster, and a bit quicker on the ball.

He may only have played about 20 minutes and it may only have been a training game, but Son was exhausted when he came off.

Nevertheless, his mind was made up. This time next year, he was going to be at their level. He was going to be in the first team.

7

INJURY

August 2010, Volksparkstadion, Hamburg, Germany
Hamburg v Chelsea

Son stood on the pitch and glanced over at the Chelsea
players, watching them going through their pre-match
stretches.

The game was only a friendly, but he was still totally
starstruck by some of the players he could see. He
already knew who Chelsea were starting, but even so
seeing them warming up on the same pitch as him took

his breath away for a moment. Frank Lampard, John Terry, Didier Drogba …

These were players he'd watched dominate the Premier League as he was growing up, and now here he was, playing against them for real. No doubt about it, this was going to be one of the biggest games that Son had ever played.

Yet he knew that, if he could carry on playing with the form he'd shown in recent games, he was almost guaranteed to be in the manager's plans for the start of the season.

He'd spent his first year after properly joining Hamburg mainly training with the youth team, only occasionally getting to train with the first team.

But now the first team had a new manager, Armin Veh, and in his first week at the club he'd approached Son.

"Son," he said, avoiding calling him "Sonny" as most of the players did. "I've had my eye on you since I got here. I want to get you in the first-team squad."

"Alright," Son said, not wanting to say anything that might change his manager's mind.

"We've got a few pre-season friendlies coming up," Veh continued, "so I'll try and give you a start as a striker. Is that alright with you?"

"Yeah," Son said, nodding. His dad had always told him that you say "Yes" to a manager's requests immediately – and then you work out later how you're going to fulfil them.

"If you do well, you'll be in a good position to start the season," Veh continued. "But don't worry if it goes badly – it won't be the end of the world and you'll still be in my plans."

Son had started pre-season in the best form of his life. He'd scored in every game and had already got nine goals.

"Sonny's going to be our secret weapon this year!" Mladen Petric̆ had announced after their last game.

And today they were playing Chelsea.

Son started the game on the bench, feeling very confident. He knew he was on top form – he felt fit and strong and he was full of energy, desperate to make his mark. He just hoped he'd get the chance to get on the pitch and prove himself today.

Chelsea were 1-0 up at half time, but in the second half Hamburg fought back hard.

Son was subbed on and then, with 18 minutes to go, Mladen Petric´ made the most of a mistake by Yury Zhirkov to beat the Chelsea keeper and level the scores.

Then, five minutes before the end of the game, Son got his chance. He nipped onto a forward pass, after a slightly lucky deflection off a defender, before skipping past Ricardo Carvalho, rolling the ball round him and driving into the box.

Son saw the keeper coming out and, without missing a step, he fired the ball beneath the keeper and into the back of the net.

GOAL!

Son was instantly mobbed by his jubilant team-mates. This wasn't just a big goal against Chelsea – it was a winning goal against the current Premier League champions, one of the best sides in the world. This was the kind of goal to secure Son's place in the first team.

"This is going to be a big year for us," Piotr Trochowski shouted. "At least, as long as you stay fit, Son," he added with a grin.

But then, as if Piotr's words were some kind of jinx, just a few minutes later Son picked up an injury to his foot. It was serious and Son instantly knew he was going to have to come off.

He just hoped that it wasn't too bad. If he got a bad injury now, then he wouldn't be starting the season in the first team. And he knew that it would be really tough to win his place back, once he'd lost it.

In fact, the news was worse than he'd anticipated.

"It's broken, kid," the physio said, looking down at Son's foot. "You'll be out for a while."

Son held his head in his hands. It was all he could do not to cry. This was supposed to be his big break, his big moment to get in the first team. He was playing the best football of his life – and now his career was on hold.

And for how long?

Armin Veh was one of the first people to come and see Son after the news had broken.

"I don't want you to worry, Son," he said. "You were one of our best players in the pre-season and I won't forget that. You'll be back in my plans as soon as you're fit again."

8

FIRST TEAM, FIRST GOAL

October 2010, RheinEnergieStadion, Köln, Germany
Köln v Hamburg

"You're starting," Veh said simply.

"Really?" Son replied, taken aback. He'd been out for two months with his foot injury and he'd only just got himself fit again.

"Yep," Veh said. "You've come back to training really well and I've been really impressed with you. We've got a couple of injuries at the moment, so I'm going to start you in the next game. You'll be playing out on the right wing."

Son nodded, lost for words. He'd been hoping to rejoin the first team once he recovered from his injury, especially after his strong performances in pre-season, but he definitely wasn't expecting to get a start in his first game back.

Son rushed home to tell his dad. They'd both been worried by Son's injury, with Son Woong-jung reminding his son how, long ago, *his* career had been cut short by a bad injury.

When his dad heard Son's news, he was even more thrilled than his son.

"You'll be one of the youngest players ever to play for Hamburg," his dad babbled, a big grin on his face.

"It might just be a one-off," Son said, tempering his dad's enthusiasm. He'd never seen his dad so excited, suddenly realising how much it meant to him for Son to be playing his first-team debut.

"Well, then you'll have to impress," his dad replied, quickly becoming serious. "*Make sure* that you're going to be a regular in the team. Force their hand."

The game was away to Köln and it got off to a lightning-quick start, with the home team taking the lead after barely ten minutes.

Son shook his head. He couldn't have his first game end in defeat.

But a few minutes later Mladen Petrić pulled Hamburg back level with a firm header from a corner.

"Welcome back, Sonny," Petrić laughed, as they celebrated the goal. "Time for *you* to get on the scoresheet now."

Now Son was determined – and it showed in his play. Every touch was perfect and he was quicker than the Köln defenders. He knew there would be chances today.

A ball over the top eluded the defenders and straight away Son was on the end of it, racing towards goal. He spotted the keeper running out and, as the ball bounced, he flicked it over the keeper's head. The ball came down just as Son went around the keeper and he volleyed it on his left foot into the net.

GOAL! Son had scored on his debut!

He ran round the corner with a finger on his lips, sprinting towards Petrić.

"On the scoresheet now, aren't I?" he laughed.

The only disappointment was that Köln eventually ran out 3-2 winners. Despite scoring, Son had ended up on the losing side on his debut.

His dad was in the dressing room at full-time, waiting for him.

"You played really well," he said, giving his son a big hug.

"I'm annoyed we lost," Son replied, kicking his boots off.

"That's the right attitude," his dad grinned. "The attitude of a winner."

Son couldn't bring himself to smile back.

"I've got some good news for you, though," his dad continued. "You're the youngest player ever to score for Hamburg in the Bundesliga!"

Despite his disappointment at the result, Son knew that today was a great day. He'd played his first ever game in the Bundesliga – a start, no less – and he'd scored, the youngest player ever to do so for his club.

But, most important, Son knew that this was just the beginning.

9

INTERNATIONAL DEBUT

January 2011, Al Gharafa Stadium, Doha, Qatar
Asian Cup, South Korea v India

Son stood on the touchline as the third official raised the electronic board and displayed Son's number in green. He was moments away from making his international debut for South Korea, against India.

As his team-mate slowly walked towards him to come off, Son found himself thinking about the events of the past few months.

His debut had impressed his team, but he'd also caught the eye of many in the Bundesliga – and back home in South Korea too.

"Everyone's talking about you," his brother told him during their weekly phone call. "They think you're going to be the next big thing."

"Well, it's early days," Son laughed.

"Yeah, that's what I said," Heung-yun scoffed. "So don't start getting too big for your boots just yet."

Nevertheless, Son was now a confirmed member of the first team and one of the best young talents in the Bundesliga. He was getting noticed.

He got the call in December, not long before the Christmas break.

"Hi. Is that Heung-Min Son?"

"Yeah," Son replied. "Who is this?"

"My name's Cho Kwang-rae. I'm the manager of South Korea."

Son was silent. He hadn't expected that. He was still just 18 – surely too young to be joining the South Korea team. He knew the 2011 Asian Cup was coming up, but even so …

Then he realised he hadn't said anything for several awkward seconds.

"Are you still there?" Cho asked, and Son could hear him laughing softly down the phone.

"Yeah, sorry," Son replied. "I'm just taking it all in."

"That's OK, I've had a few conversations like this," Cho chuckled. "I suspect you know why I'm calling. I want you in my squad for the friendlies at the end of December – and then for the Asian Cup next year."

"For the Cup?" Son asked, trying to contain his excitement.

"Yeah. Is that alright?" Cho replied.

"Yeah. I mean, I think so," Son said, still reeling.

"Take a few days to consider it," Cho continued. "It will mean you missing a chunk of the season with Hamburg, and I know you're just getting into the team, so it's a big commitment."

After the call, Son thought about the offer. There was only one person he trusted to help him decide – his dad.

Son Woong-jung had always said that it was important to focus on your club first, as sometimes the distraction of the national team could be detrimental to a player's career.

"I think you should go," his dad had told him.

"Really?"

"Yeah. It would be a great experience," his dad had said. "You might not play that much, so there's no real risk of injury – and who knows whether you'll get this kind of opportunity in the future."

Son nodded. As soon as his dad had said "Yes", he realised that he was desperate to play. He'd just been waiting for his dad to agree.

Now Son was on the bench, watching South Korea march into a 3-1 lead against India in the last group game of the Asian Cup.

He felt sure that this had to be his chance – and he was right. Cho approached him at half-time.

"I'm getting you on for the second half," he said. "The game's probably won, so I just want to see what you can do. Go out and get a goal or two."

Son just nodded. He knew what he had to do. He might only be eighteen, but he wanted to be a regular for South Korea. This was his chance.

He started well, terrorising the Indian defence. He was quicker and more skilful than the Indian players and they couldn't handle him. Once more, he sensed goals.

After a few minutes, he fired a shot that rattled off the post and out of play.

"Come on, man," he said, laughing to himself. He couldn't believe he hadn't scored with that one.

A moment later, he was slipped through by Koo Ja-Cheol. This time, Son didn't bother with a touch, simply striking the ball first-time as hard as he could. He watched it whistle into the top-left corner of the goal.

GOAL!

He ran over to the fans, a big smile on his face.

"That's your first international goal, right?" asked Koo, running up behind him.

"First of many, I reckon," Ji-Sung Park added, as they jogged back to the half-way line.

Son couldn't believe it. He had just made his debut in a major international tournament, and he'd scored as well.

First goal in his first appearance – it was becoming a habit.

10
NOT FAIR

March 2012, Son's home, Hamburg, Germany

"He's just not picking me," Son moaned. "And we're not even playing that well – so I don't know why he just won't give me a chance."

Son looked across to his dad, who was sitting on the sofa, listening to his son.

It had been a crazy eighteen months for Son. He'd gone from being an unknown in both Germany and

South Korea to now being the shining light in both countries.

The South Korean team had gone all the way through to the semi-finals of the Asian Cup, before a devastating penalty shoot-out defeat to Japan.

Son had found it hard to pick himself up after that loss. He hadn't been able to control his emotions at the full-time whistle, collapsing in floods of tears. He'd known that this wasn't his last chance to win a trophy, but at the time it had certainly felt like it.

And, to make matters worse, in the rest of the season he'd only played six more times for Hamburg.

A couple of manager changes had pushed him a lot further down the pecking order. Armin Veh had been replaced by Michael Oenning, and he'd been replaced in turn by the new manager, Thorsten Fink.

Fink was a little unsure about Son at first and didn't play him for the first couple of games. It was only after a hard-fought 2-2 draw against Bayer Leverkusen that Fink seemed to be won over.

He'd singled Son out for a talk in the training session on the Monday after the Leverkusen game.

"You normally play as a winger, don't you, Sonny?" he'd said, looking Son up and down.

"Yeah, but I'm happy to play anywhere!" Son had said eagerly, keen to impress the new manager.

"Yeah, alright," Fink had replied, a little taken aback by Son's energy. "I think I might have a new role for you. I'm thinking of playing you as a striker alongside Guerrero," he'd continued. "You'll have to work hard and press the defenders – you might not get a lot of chances yourself, but it will really help the team."

Son had nodded again. He was always happy to do something that would help the team, even if it meant he didn't get any individual prizes.

But even after he'd played a huge part in a crucial 1–1 draw with Bayern Munich, Son still spent most of the season on the bench.

Which is why he'd asked his dad to come over for a chat.

"You're going to have to impress him," his dad said to Son, after listening to his complaints. "Take your chances when you're given the opportunity. Remember – you have to prove that you belong."

"But I have!" Son complained. "I've done all that! It's just not *fair*."

"Don't complain about it not being *fair*," his dad cut in. "There's no reason why he has to pick you. If he isn't, it's because there's a reason. It might just be that he doesn't like you, or it might be something else."

Son Woong-jung gave his son a steely look. "You have to play well enough to give him *no choice*. Even if he hates you, he *has* to pick you."

Son didn't reply. He was frustrated at the whole situation – and now he was annoyed that his dad hadn't just taken his side.

He wanted his dad to back him up, but instead of that he'd just gone ahead and made a number of sensible points.

Son stared at the floor for a few minutes, thinking it all over.

His dad was right. Son was going to have to give the manager *no option* but to play him.

"OK," he said finally. "I'll make it so he'll *have* to pick me."

II
NO OPTION

April 2012, Volksparkstadion, Hamburg, Germany
Hamburg v Hannover

The atmosphere in the dressing room before the game was tense. Son and his team-mates were fully focused on the job they had to do.

This was a huge game for Hamburg. They'd had a disappointing season and were at real risk of being relegated to the second division. Today they were at home to Hannover and were desperate for some points.

For this game Thorsten Fink had handed Son a rare start up front, alongside Marcus Berg.

He was taking a risk starting Son, given that he hadn't played him much throughout the season, but the manager was running out of options.

For Son, this was the time to impress, just as his dad said. *Give the manager no choice but to play you.*

"I'll handle the centre-backs," Berg said to Son before the game. "I'll try and give you the space to cause some damage."

Son just nodded.

He could sense the nervous atmosphere amongst the fans as the team walked out onto the pitch. The stadium was full, but much quieter than usual.

Son had been so consumed with his own personal drama that it hadn't really occurred to him that Hamburg might actually go down this year. Now the nervous crowd brought home how important this match was.

Son started the game well, quickly causing Hannover problems. His pace and his quick footwork were panicking the defenders, and after 12 minutes he got his first chance.

He got the ball on the left-hand side, skipping past the defender and driving into the box. For a moment it looked as though the chance had gone, but Son held onto the ball. Holding back the defender, he wrapped his right foot around the ball, curling it towards goal.

GOAL! 1-0!

"Come on!" he roared, as the whole team surrounded him. Under normal circumstances a goal like that wouldn't have merited such a huge celebration. But now the club's survival was on the line – and that goal really mattered.

The rest of the game was tense and nervy. Son spent more time chasing defenders than he did with the ball, but he did enough. His important work had been after those opening 12 minutes. Hamburg had won 1-0 and taken a giant step towards safety.

At the final whistle, Son walked off the pitch feeling satisfied. He'd got some valuable points for his club, but he'd also shown his manager that, if he gave him some game time, Son could deliver.

Now, perhaps, Thorsten Fink might realise that he had no option but to play him.

12

WISE WORDS

September 2012, Hamburg training ground,
Hamburg, Germany

"I was impressed with your work last season, Sonny,"
Thorsten Fink said with a smile. "But now let's see if we
can get you a few more goals."

"How should we do that?" Son asked, once more
eager to learn.

"You've already got a good technique," Fink replied.
"I think a tip that I could give you is try and shoot early

– catch the keeper off-guard, before he can set himself."

"Yeah," Son said, looking around as if he'd like a notebook to write it down in.

"Work with Rafa," Fink continued, gesturing towards van der Vaart, who was warming up on the training pitch. "He's scored goals wherever he's been. If anyone can help you, it'll be him."

Son nodded. He'd been looking forward to speaking to Rafael van der Vaart anyway. The man was a legend – and not just at Hamburg. He'd even played in a World Cup final.

There had been a lot of change at Hamburg over the summer. The club had dodged relegation by the skin of its teeth, largely thanks to Son's crucial goals at the end of the season, and now they had their sights set firmly on getting back into Europe.

Van der Vaart had returned to Hamburg from Spurs, to much fanfare, and at the same time Mladen Petric had left the club. Fink was making it clear that Son was now his main man.

It took a lot of courage for Son to approach van der Vaart. Rafa had a relaxed air about him and it was rare to see him hanging around on the training ground after a session.

Son didn't want to be the one to bother him, to force him to train more than he wanted to – but eventually he did manage to catch him one day, just before he left the ground.

"Hey, Rafa!" he called, sounding nervous. "I was wondering if I could have a chat with you about something."

"Sure, Sonny." Rafa turned and smiled, instantly putting Son at ease.

"The gaffer wants me to try and score a few more goals this year," Son continued, "and ... like ... I know you've scored goals everywhere, so I didn't know if you had some tips or anything ... "

"Yeah, alright," Rafa replied.

The next day, the two of them met up on the training ground and Rafa began to talk Son through some of the things that he'd done over his long career at the top.

Son grabbed a few balls and got ready to practise, but van der Vaart waved them away.

"Put those away," he said. "We don't need them."

Son left them and slowly walked over to Rafa. How was he going to teach him to score goals without a football?

"Most of finishing is mental," Rafa said, tapping the side of his head. "It's all very well being quick and having great ability, but if you get in the right position and then you panic, or if you think of the wrong thing – it's useless."

Son nodded.

"You've got to be aware of your opposition as well," Rafa continued. "If they've got a massive centre-back, then you don't try and compete with him in the air. Take him on the ground, where you're probably quicker than him anyway."

Rafa paused, looking directly at Son. "If their right back is quick, but their left back is slow – then you take on the slow one."

"Yeah," Son said. He knew about that tip.

"I think the most important thing is never to overthink it," Rafa continued. "You get the opportunity, you shoot. If you miss, then you try again next time. Don't try and think about what the keeper's going to do, or where he's going to dive – just put your foot through it."

"So don't try and aim for the corners or anything?" Son asked.

"*I* don't," Rafa replied curtly. "If you've practised enough, then you should be able to hit them on instinct, without thinking."

Son nodded. This wasn't quite the fool-proof advice that he'd wanted to hear. He'd been hoping to hear something that would guarantee him goals.

Nevertheless, he understood what Rafa was telling him. You couldn't guarantee anything, but being physically and mentally in the right place at the right time made goals much more likely.

Having van der Vaart in the team was definitely proving useful in other ways too. The opposition defenders were obsessed with him, which left Son with so much more space.

He started the season in prolific form, with six goals in his opening 12 games, including a brace against Dortmund.

Hamburg had improved massively on the previous

season and they were now in a real race to finish in the top six.

And in Son and van der Vaart they had two of the best players in the league. The combination of van der Vaart's touch and passing ability and Son's blistering pace were causing opposition defences all sorts of problems.

Son was happy to do the defensive work as well, an eagerness that came from his upbringing and from his dad's emphasis on putting the team first.

That had all helped to get him into the team in the first place, and he wasn't going to let up now. It just wasn't in his nature.

But being a key player in a team that was pressing at the very top of the league wasn't enough for Son. He was desperate to prove that he wasn't just a hot prospect, or one to look out for in the future.

He was one for the present. He wanted to see results now.

13

SUPERSTAR

February 2013, Signal Iduna Park, Dortmund, Germany
Borussia Dortmund v Hamburg

Van der Vaart chuckled. "You nervous, Sonny?"

"A little bit," Son confessed. "It's tense out there."

"Don't worry about them," Rafael laughed again. "Once you get out there and it's just you and the ball – that's all that matters. You won't even notice them then."

Hamburg were away at Dortmund, a team they'd

already beaten this season, but playing Dortmund on their home ground was a very different game.

There were over 80,000 fans in the stadium and the legendary Dortmund "Yellow Wall" loomed large.

Son had never experienced an atmosphere like this. It was ominous, and in the dressing room most of the players seemed nervous. The only man who looked unfazed was Rafa.

As the players lined up to walk out onto the pitch, the songs and chants of the crowd were like a wall of noise. The tunnel amplified the already deafening fans, and it only seemed to be getting louder.

But Rafa was right. As soon as Son got out onto the turf, he forgot where he was. He didn't even notice the thousands of screaming fans who were roaring at him. All that mattered now was getting the ball and trying to score.

The game started poorly with Robert Lewandowski poking Dortmund in front. But just moments later Artjoms Rudņevs equalised for Hamburg.

They were back in it.

"Ignore the fact that these are the champions, lads!"

van der Vaart shouted. "We beat them at home and we can do it again here!"

Then Rafa turned to Son. "Sonny, just remember what we talked about – don't overthink it!"

Son got his first chance a few minutes later, when he was played in and was able to go round the keeper. But he was forced wide and when he managed to get his shot off it smashed into the post.

Remembering Rafa's advice, he picked himself up and got back into the game, focusing on when his next chance would come.

Sure enough, it wasn't long before that chance came. He picked up the ball on the right-hand side, driving at the Dortmund defence. Then he cut in on his left foot and decided to let fly.

The ball whistled through the air like a rocket and nestled in the far corner of the goal, leaving the keeper stranded.

GOAL! Now Hamburg had the lead.

Not long before half-time the game changed when Lewandowski was sent off for a rash challenge. The rest of the match was a bad-tempered, feisty affair and

Hamburg's centre-back Jeffrey Bruma was sent off in the second half.

Dortmund kept pushing hard for an equaliser but just minutes later Rudņevs poked Hamburg further ahead. Now it was 3-1.

They were running away with it.

"Stay at the back post when he crosses," van der Vaart shouted over to Son, pointing at the left-back Marcell Jansen. "They're not picking you up and it will come through."

With just a few moments left to play, that's exactly what happened. Jansen fizzed the ball into the box and Son was there, lurking at the back. He tapped it in.

GOAL! 4-1!

Son wheeled away to celebrate his goal – and the win – with the fans who'd made the trip to Dortmund. Hamburg hadn't just *beaten* the champions – they'd thrashed them.

There was no doubt about it now. Son was in flying form. He was no longer a hot prospect – he was a superstar.

Now everyone in Germany had their eyes on him.

14
NEW CLUB

June 2013, BayArena Stadium, Leverkusen, Germany

"Hey, Son, over here!" called out one of the photographers. He needn't have bothered, as Son couldn't hear him over all the commotion and the noise of the cameras.

Everyone just wanted a shot of Son holding up his new Bayer Leverkusen shirt.

Son and van der Vaart had been on top form in the

previous season, but Hamburg had only managed to finish seventh in the league and they'd missed out on Europe.

But Son's form had attracted attention from some of the biggest clubs in Europe, including fellow German club Bayer Leverkusen.

And in early June his agent had confirmed the news. Leverkusen had made an offer for him and Hamburg had accepted it.

The only question now was – did Son want to go?

He had a lot to think about. Hamburg were the team who'd given him his first opportunities – didn't he owe them some loyalty?

And even if he moved, were Leverkusen the right club for him? And then, if he did join them, would he even get to play in the first team?

Once more, he turned to his dad for advice.

"You're overthinking it," his dad said simply. "The truth is, you don't owe Hamburg anything. They've accepted the bid anyway, so they're happy to go along with it."

"But will I play at Leverkusen?" Son asked. His dad

had always stressed how important it was for a player to be at the right club, and game time was vital. There was no point spending a season on the bench.

"Have you not been following the news?" his dad asked him. "They're about to sell André Schürrle to Chelsea. You're clearly the replacement – they've obviously signed you for the first team."

Son listened carefully. His dad had always been naturally cautious, especially when it came to football. On top of that, his own experiences as a player in the distant past had made him particularly wary. But now even his dad thought that this was the right decision.

It was the middle of June when the move was confirmed – a record fee for Bayer Leverkusen.

His dad had been right as, a couple of weeks later, André Schürrle departed for Chelsea.

For Son, Leverkusen's biggest selling point was the Champions League. That was the biggest club competition in the world and only the best of the best were in it. Leverkusen were regulars in the competition, and Son couldn't wait to get the chance to play in it.

Son was immediately working with higher quality

players at Leverkusen, and this was obvious in the early training sessions.

Bernd Leno was one of the best keepers in Germany, and Emre Can and Gonzalo Castro were playing passes he couldn't even dream of. Not to mention Stefan Kiessling, who had been one of the top scorers in the Bundesliga over the last five years.

Then, just as Son joined the team, manager Sami Hyypiä made it clear what he was expecting in the coming season.

"We've been in the top four for a while now, lads," he said. "Now it's time to take that next step – I want the title this year."

There were several murmurs amongst the players. Some weren't sure about his ambition, as Bayern Munich looked invincible, having just won the treble.

Whatever some of his team-mates might think, Son couldn't wait for the challenge. He was currently at the top of his game, a star player at a top club that was aiming for the league title – and with half an eye on the Champions League as well. Everything seemed perfectly set up for success.

"I want to play in England next," Son told his brother when they spoke that week on the phone.

Son knew that the tempo of the English game and the passion in the stands were like nothing else. There was a reason why the Premier League was the best league in the world.

"Steady on, bro," Heung-yun laughed. "You've only just got to Leverkusen – you can't be thinking about a move already!"

Son knew that Heung-yun was right, but no matter – his mind was already made up.

One day, he was going to make the move to the Premier League.

15

"GOING EASY"

November 2013, BayArena Stadium, Leverkusen, Germany
Bayer Leverkusen vs Hamburg

"Go easy on us today, Sonny," van der Vaart laughed, as he stood facing Son in the tunnel.

Today Leverkusen were playing Son's old team Hamburg – and, as van der Vaart knew, Son didn't know how to "go easy".

He got his first chance in the first ten minutes of the game. Gonzalo Castro slipped the ball into him and he skipped past the keeper and slammed the ball into the back of the net.

Son didn't really celebrate this goal though – he just raised his hands, showing respect to his old team. But as the game restarted, he continued playing as hard as ever.

He was played in again by Sidney Sam and raced past the defenders. He saw the keeper rushing out, determined not to be beaten this time.

But Son kept running, taking the ball with him around the keeper. He almost stumbled, but managed to stay on his feet, poking the ball into the goal.

Again Son kept his celebrations quiet, but under his mask he was bursting and bubbling with energy. He now had an opportunity to get a hat-trick. It was just a shame it might come against his former club.

But Hamburg weren't going down easily. Two goals either side of half-time brought them level, and now Leverkusen had a fight on their hands.

Fortunately for his team, Son was in the form of his life. Five minutes after Hamburg equalised, he found the ball at his feet on the edge of the box.

He didn't have time to think as instinct just kicked in. He controlled the ball, moved into the box and, before the keeper even had a chance to set himself, he whipped it into the far corner.

GOAL!

He did celebrate this one, his third, allowing himself just a fist bump and a wry smile.

Then back to business – there was still a lot of the match left to play.

"You need to try and get four now," Stefan Kiessling chuckled. "Or at least let me get one!"

Son did help Kiessling get one not long after, laying the ball off to the big striker, who poked it past the keeper. That made it 4-2 – and the game was surely won.

Although there were still a few final twists, in the end Leverkusen ran out 5-3 winners.

Son almost didn't care about the final score. It was his first hat-trick in professional football, and he was sure it wouldn't be his last.

He was just 20 years old and everything just seemed to keep on going his way.

16
OUT WIDE?

January 2015, Bayer Leverkusen training ground,
Leverkusen, Germany

"I think you should be aiming for 20 goals this year," new Leverkusen manager Roger Schmidt told him, on his first day in the job. "You had a great season last year," he continued, "but I think you can really kick on this year."

"Am I playing as a striker, then?" Son asked, surprise showing on his face.

Son's first season at Leverkusen had been a huge success. He'd been a regular in a Leverkusen team that had been in the top two for most of the season. They'd ultimately finished fourth, but it had still been an impressive achievement.

He'd half-hoped there would be some interest from clubs in the Premier League, but no offers had arrived. Instead, Leverkusen's manager Sami Hyypiä had been sacked and replaced by Roger Schmidt.

Schmidt was more reserved than Hyypiä, but even so he was already singling out Son for praise.

But was Schmidt now telling him he wanted him playing up front?

"No, I want you to play out on the left," Schmidt continued. "Kiessling is going to be our main striker."

"How am I going to get 20 goals from out there?" Son asked, without really thinking.

He didn't mean to disrespect the manager, but he just couldn't see how he was going to score that many goals from out wide.

"Think of Ronaldo," Schmidt said. "He plays out on the left for Real Madrid and he scores 40 or 50 goals a year. It's all about timing your runs and being in the right place at the right time."

Even so, Son knew it was going to be hard to get the goals target Schmidt had set him. Ronaldo was one of the best players of all time – and he did a fraction of the defensive work that Son had to do.

Leverkusen started the season in good form, easing through their Champions League group and once more finding themselves near the top of the league. But costly draws against some of the smaller sides meant they were way off the pace.

"There's no way we're ever going to catch Bayern," Kiessling remarked.

Son had to agree. Bayern were completely untouchable at the moment and it looked as if the league title was already out of their reach.

Perhaps the Asian Cup would give Son his biggest opportunity this year.

17

SO CLOSE

January 2015, Stadium Australia, Sydney, Australia
2015 Asian Cup Final – South Korea v Australia

"We beat them in the group stage, guys," South Korea's new German manager, Uli Stielike, reminded them in the dressing room. "There's no reason why we can't do the same again here."

Today was the Asian Cup Final – with South Korea playing the hosts, Australia. The stadium in Sydney was rammed, with Australians making up most of the crowd.

Unlike four years ago, Son was now a key player in the team – and today he was captain as well.

"We've been the best team at this tournament," Son said to the lads, surprising himself with his confidence. "So let's go out and win this today!"

As they walked out, Son couldn't avoid eyeing up the trophy that stood at the end of the tunnel. This was the closest he'd come to a trophy in his professional career. If they won today, they'd be legends in South Korea.

The two teams were evenly matched, with both Tim Cahill and Son coming close to opening the scoring. Overall South Korea were the better side and Australia had to work hard to stop them going ahead.

But moments before half-time, Australia struck. A ball into the feet of Massimo Luongo allowed the Australian to turn and fire a shot past the despairing dive of South Korean keeper Kim Jin-hyeon.

The noise from the Australian crowd was huge, and Son felt he could barely hear himself think. It was the first goal that the South Koreans had conceded in the tournament and their heads immediately started to drop.

The second half was a hard slog and South Korea couldn't find a way to break down the stubborn Australian defence. They were starting to make a number of uncharacteristic mistakes too – the pressure no doubt starting to get to them.

"Come on, lads!" Son roared, trying to encourage both the team and himself on. He led by example, taking players on, firing shots off, keeping up the pressure.

The game ticked past the ninetieth minute and into added time. South Korea badly needed a goal.

Suddenly they found a bit of space, with Ki Sung-yueng poking the ball into Son's path. A moment later, Son was in the box.

The game seemed to freeze around him. Now it was just Son and the keeper. Now he was running on instinct.

Just as van der Vaart had told him all those years ago, he didn't aim for the corners, he didn't overthink it or try to be clever. He just let his feet go as he took a touch and smashed it past the keeper.

"Yes, Sonny!" Ki roared, as Son was mobbed by his team-mates.

"Quick, guys!" Son replied, pushing his team-mates away. "One more! Let's win this in extra time!"

Extra time was frenetic, with both exhausted teams pushing for a winner. But it was Australia who got the breakthrough, when Tomi Juric smuggled the ball to the feet of James Troisi, who smashed it home.

Son collapsed to his knees, feeling the tears welling up. Surely he wasn't going to miss out on a trophy again, especially after coming so close, after walking past it just before the game.

There were still fifteen minutes of the game left and Son tried to drag himself up and keep going. He couldn't give up yet.

But it wasn't enough. Australia won the match 2-1 and were crowned champions of Asia.

South Korea had come so close, but ultimately they were going home trophy-less.

This was a hard loss – the hardest yet in Son's career. It took a lot out of him to return to Leverkusen, and their desperate pursuit of the Bundesliga, without a winner's medal around his neck.

18
MOVE

June 2015, Son's home, Leverkusen, Germany

"I want to move," Son told his dad. "I think it's time."

"Are you sure?" Son Woong-jung asked him. "You're in a good place at Leverkusen. You could always do another few seasons there."

"I just think I've gone as far as I can there," Son replied. "We were fourth in the league again this season. We're never going to catch Bayern – and I want to win trophies."

"So, where do you want to go?" his dad asked.

"I want the Premier League," Son said simply.

Son still remembered the first Champions League game he'd played for Leverkusen, against Manchester United. They'd lost 4-2, but he'd never forgotten the pace of the game, or the passion of the Man U fans. From that moment he'd always known that his next move would be to England.

"You'll need to speak to your agent, then," his dad replied. "See if he can set up a move for you."

Son agreed, and a few days later he informed the club. Leverkusen were quick to remind him that any move would need a price tag of at least 20 million euros. Any less and Son wouldn't be able to leave.

No offers came in during June or July, and Son was beginning to accept that he was going to be at Leverkusen for another season. Then he got the call.

"We've got an offer for you," his agent said.

"Is it the Prem?" Son asked, praying desperately that it was going to be a team from England.

"Yep," his agent said, pausing slightly. "It's Tottenham Hotspur."

Son hesitated. He'd heard of Tottenham – he knew they were in London and he knew they were quite big.

But his worry was that they were too similar to his current club. Like Leverkusen, Spurs hadn't won a trophy in a long time. Did he really have a chance to win the league with them?

But then Spurs manager Mauricio Pochettino got in touch with him. He was passionate about Tottenham's chances of winning the league, or at the very least a domestic cup, and he was able to convince Son that he could be the difference for Spurs.

The move was eventually sealed at the end of August for 30 million euros – a record fee for an Asian player. If Son wasn't already a major celebrity in South Korea, he definitely was now.

Nevertheless, he was under no illusions. The Premier League was tough and he knew for sure that this move wouldn't be easy.

But it was exactly what he'd wanted. Now he was in the best league in the world, with a chance at trophies and the opportunity to take his game to the next level.

He couldn't wait.

19
UNHAPPY

June 2016, Tottenham Hotspur training ground,
London, England

"Hey, boss." Son tapped on the door of Pochettino's office. "I was wondering if I could have a quick chat with you about something."

The pace and ferociousness of the Premier League had been a shock for Son, and it had taken him a while to get used to it.

He had less space than he did in the Bundesliga and

often struggled to get in the game. Every time he got the ball a defender would instantly be challenging him hard.

His first home game had been against Crystal Palace, when Pochettino had played him at number 10, just behind Kane.

It was in the second half that Son had got his chance. He'd got the ball about 30 yards out and run at the defence. Worried about tackling him, they'd backed off, allowing him to skip into the box before driving a left-footed shot past the keeper.

Son had scored in his first home game. The crowd had erupted into huge cheers, everyone delighted for their new man.

"Welcome to White Hart Lane, Sonny!" Harry Kane had roared as they'd celebrated.

His career at Spurs couldn't have got off to a better start, but as the weeks passed things had not been so positive.

Son had spent a lot of time on the bench, as Spurs had one of their best seasons in recent history.

He'd even started to question whether he really belonged in the Premier League.

So he had decided to speak to the Spurs manager about his worries. He didn't want to stir up trouble, but he couldn't spend another year as a back-up option.

"You're not happy with your playing time," Pochettino said, smiling at Son. He already knew what the conversation was going to be about.

"Yeah," Son said. "I was just thinking about maybe trying to get a move or something. I don't want things to carry on like this."

Pochettino stood up from behind his desk and came over to Son, gesturing for him to sit down on the chair in the office.

"Look, Sonny, we don't want to lose you," he said, sitting down next to him. "I think there's definitely a role for you here."

"But I don't know how long I can wait," Son replied. He didn't want to wait years, just for a chance to play in the team.

"It takes time for anyone to adapt to this league," Pochettino said calmly. "It's different to anywhere else in the world."

Son nodded.

"I think you'd regret it if you left now," Pochettino continued. "You don't get a lot of opportunities to have a crack at the Premier League. At least give it one more season."

Son hesitated. "I don't know … "

"OK, how about this?" Poch said. "Stay until January. That's six months. If you're still not happy then, we'll look to sort out a move for you. Deal?"

He stuck out his hand.

Son hesitated. He trusted Pochettino and he knew he was a man of his word. The fact that the club were so desperate to keep him was a good sign. If they really didn't rate him, then they'd have just let him go. So he was sure there was a real opportunity for him to get in the Spurs team.

"We'll need you if we're going to win the title this year," Poch said, laying out his ambitions.

"Alright," Son said, reaching out and shaking the manager's hand.

20
TURNING POINT?

September 2016, Bet365 Stadium, Stoke, England
Stoke v Tottenham Hotspur

"We're going for an attacking front four," Pochettino announced, showing the team sheet, which listed Son, Kane, Alli and Christian Eriksen up front.

"Welcome back, Sonny," Dele said, slapping him on the back.

Son had returned from the summer break to a warm welcome from his team-mates and the staff at the club.

He had real friends here and, although his desire to play wasn't always being met, he was glad it was Spurs he was returning to after the break.

They knew the game against Stoke today would be tough, and the first half was tense and nervy as Spurs tried to get comfortable playing in their new shape.

"When Christian gets it out wide, you hang back on the edge of the box," Kane said to Son during a break in play. "The defenders will mark me and you'll have all the space."

Son nodded. He trusted Kane's instincts – he was a great player and Son looked up to him. Son knew too that his team-mates were desperate to help him get his first goal in the Premier League.

Just before half-time, the moment arrived. Kane had been right – the defenders stuck tightly to him and left Son with space in the middle of the box.

"Christian!" Son bellowed. "Here!"

The ball from Eriksen was perfect, as usual. Son just needed to poke it in with his left foot. He didn't make the cleanest connection, but it was enough to take it past the keeper.

GOAL!

He was off the mark for the new season.

With the score now 1-0, Stoke had to come and attack if they wanted anything from the game, and that would leave more space behind their defence. With Spurs' attacking line-up this would leave Stoke vulnerable at the back, and Son knew that they could exploit this.

"This is perfect for you, Sonny," Kane said, coming over to him. "They can't match your pace so, if you go for it, you'll be free."

Once more it was Christian Eriksen who set Son up, timing his run perfectly.

Erikson slipped a ball through the defence and Son was away. He was in the box, out on the left and he didn't bother to take a touch first – he just whipped it with his right foot into the top corner.

"I don't know how he managed that!" Eriksen laughed.

"I don't think the Premier League is ready for this front four!" Dele Alli shouted, joining in the celebrations.

Alli and Kane added two more goals, as Spurs ran out emphatic 4-0 winners.

It may not have been a cup final, or a massive game against the champions, but this win felt just as big to Son.

The chemistry between himself, Kane, Eriksen and Alli had been brilliant throughout the game. Son felt that they were meant to play together.

He felt too that this match was a turning point. With two goals to his credit, now, finally, he was ready for the Premier League.

21
CHEMISTRY

January 2017, Tottenham Hotspur training ground,
London, England

"So what are you thinking, Son? You still want a transfer?" Pochettino asked with a cheeky smile.

"Nah," Son laughed, "I think I'll stick around for a bit longer."

The win against Stoke had set the tone for the rest of the season. Son was now firmly part of Spurs' "fab four" and they were leading the line.

He scored important goals against Middlesbrough and Man City to put Spurs near the top of the league. He even won the Premier League Player of the Month award for September and for April.

Son was now one of the leading players in the league and he was playing some of the best football of his career. The decision to stay at Spurs felt totally right.

Son's chemistry with Kane had helped cement his place in the Spurs line-up, and it was a big part of why Son had decided to stay at the club. The two players had also formed a good partnership, both on and off the pitch.

"Fancy another session, Sonny?" Kane said to him after training one day.

They'd got in the habit of practising together after training sessions. They both seemed to know how each other thought, and the combination of Son's pace and Kane's finishing had proved deadly throughout the season.

They practised exchanging one-on-ones with each other, then alternately firing shots at the goal.

"How do you get so much power?" Son asked, marvelling as Kane almost broke the net with a thunderous effort.

"I don't know," Kane shrugged. "I guess it's just practice. It's like asking how you are so quick."

"I'm not *that* quick," Son laughed.

"You're quicker than most of the defenders we come up against," Kane grinned. "Look, let's do something different. I'll play the passes and you run on and try and score."

"Christian normally does the passes," Son said.

"Yeah, but I want to be able to do it too."

Son was impressed. Kane was always trying to improve his game. Never satisfied with just being a prolific finisher, he wanted more.

"Alright, but then I'm only shooting with my left foot," Son replied with a grin. He wasn't going to be outdone by Kane. They could both learn new skills.

They were out until it was dark, swapping and rotating roles, firing shots into the top corner, bottom corner, down the middle, everywhere.

Son was exhausted but happy when they finally got off the pitch. It was just like being back at home with his brother or his dad – each of them pushing the other to new levels.

22
PERFECT PARTNERSHIP

May 2017, King Power Stadium, Leicester, England

Leicester v Spurs

"Hey, Sonny," Harry Kane called, as he stood behind Son in the dressing room. "I'm not far behind in the golden boot race – you couldn't give me a hand getting some goals, could you?"

"Sure," Son replied, laughing, "if you set me up with some as well."

"Right lads," Poch said, grabbing their attention

before they left the dressing room. "We're playing for pride here – so let's finish the season with a bang!"

Today's game was away at Leicester and, although the title was now out of reach for Spurs, they wanted to end the season strongly and send out a message for next season.

They'd been knocked out of the FA Cup by Chelsea, out of the League Cup by Liverpool and they were now out of Europe.

For all that, Spurs were on for a record-breaking season, having won 12 of their last 13 games. With a couple of games left, they were already on 80 points. In any other season that would have been enough for the title, but this year Chelsea were already way out of reach.

Spurs started the game well and got their first chance inside 25 minutes, when Son found himself clear, racing into the Leicester box. He saw the keeper coming out and started lining up the shot for the far corner.

Then, out of the corner of his eye, he spotted Kane desperately racing after him and, remembering what Harry had said in the dressing room, he cut the ball back for Kane to slam it home.

GOAL!

"Cheers, Sonny!" Kane smiled, grabbing him immediately.

"How many do you need?" Son asked.

"Two more!" Kane shouted, and Son could see him sprinting back to the half-way line, more determined than ever.

Son wasn't able to set Kane up for the next Spurs goal, which he volleyed in himself after being flicked in by Dele Alli.

Kane and Son now had one each and Spurs were 2-0 up. Son shrugged in apology at his strike partner, who just laughed it off.

In the second half there was a goal from Ben Chilwell for Leicester, then Kane added another for Spurs before Son sealed the win with his second goal.

It was Harry Kane who set him up for that one, taking the defenders away with a diverting run, allowing Son to cut back onto his right foot and whip a shot into the far corner.

"You'd better not be taking my goals!" Kane laughed.

With Spurs now 4-1 up and with another game in a

few days, Son was taken off. He watched the rest of the match from the bench.

Kane probably could have done with a rest too, but Pochettino didn't dare take him off when he was chasing goals like this.

Son could only watch from the bench in amazement as Kane scored twice more, to take his tally for the match to four goals.

That meant that he leapfrogged Romelu Lukaku in the goalscoring rankings to go top.

"You've got to be happy, eh?" Son laughed, as Kane came off the pitch, celebrating the 6-1 win. "Golden boot in the bag?"

"Not yet, mate," Kane said with a determined look. "There's still a game left to go."

He marched off towards the dressing room with the match ball tucked under one arm. Son followed after him, knowing that together they made a perfect partnership.

With players like this in the team, Son was in the right place. It was only a matter of time before they won something.

23
TROPHY

September 2018, Pakansari Stadium, Cibinong, Indonesia
2018 Asian Games Cup Final – South Korea v Japan

"Come on guys," Son shouted to his South Korean team-mates who were sitting nervously in the dressing room. "We can win this!"

Once again, Son found himself playing with South Korea in the final of a major tournament. This was a huge moment – but this time it wasn't just about the trophy.

In South Korea everybody had to do mandatory military service, and the only way that Son – and the rest of the team – would be able to avoid it was if he did well in a tournament.

So winning this Asian Games Cup Final was Son's best chance of avoiding the call-up. If South Korea lost, the players would each lose 18 months of their careers to the military.

Son had never felt pressure like this before.

They were taking on Japan, one of their biggest rivals.

As Son led the team out, his heart was beating hard in his chest. He knew what was on the line here and what he had to do.

The game was tense and both teams were struggling to break down each other's defences.

As it turned out the full ninety minutes passed without goals, so the game went to extra time.

"We get one goal and we win this, lads!" Son said, trying to spur on the younger lads in the team.

And South Korea did get that goal. Son dribbled into the box, skipping past the defenders, before the ball was taken from him by Lee Seung-woo, who thrashed it into the top corner.

They doubled their lead when Hwang Hee-chan headed home from Son's cross. South Korea now had a two-goal lead and there was no way they were going to throw that away.

Japan got a goal back, but it was too little too late. Minutes later, South Korea had won the trophy.

It was Son's first ever trophy, and the feeling of finally getting his hands on one was electric.

It was greater than anything he'd ever felt in football, and it felt especially sweet to be the main man leading his national side to glory. Being the player who provided the assists for both goals made it even better.

He didn't even care about the fact that he no longer had to do military service.

After the initial euphoria had worn off, Son promised himself that that wasn't going to be the last trophy he lifted.

24
CHAMPIONS LEAGUE

April 2019, Etihad Stadium, Manchester, England
Man City v Spurs

"We know we can score goals against this team," Poch said. "We did it last week and we can do it again today. We've got the advantage now, so let's make sure it stays that way. This is a competition we can really win."

Spurs were through to the Champions League quarter-finals, having beaten Dortmund in the last sixteen. Today was the second leg of their quarter-final fixture against Man City, and Spurs were carrying a one-goal lead from the previous leg, thanks to Son.

But today was going to be tough, as Spurs were playing without Harry Kane, who'd picked up an injury.

"Pressure's on you today, Sonny," Jan Vertonghen told him. "You'll need to get the goals today."

The game started badly when Raheem Sterling curled City in front after just three minutes.

But a few minutes later Son got his chance, when a poor blocked clearance fell straight to his feet. He didn't have time to take a touch, so he swung a foot at it and fired it towards goal. It caught Ederson off guard and landed in the back of the net.

GOAL!

"Who needs Harry Kane, huh?" Dele Alli laughed.

"City need two more now to win!" Trippier shouted. An away goal was crucial in ties like this, and now Spurs had a massive advantage.

Two minutes later, Spurs got another. Christian Eriksen got the ball after good work by Lucas Moura and threaded it through to Son.

He took one touch to get the ball out from under his

feet and then curled it with his right foot. As soon as it left his foot he knew it was going in.

GOAL! 2-1!

"They're going to have to get three more now!" Trippier roared.

But it was only two minutes later that City were back level, when Bernardo Silva scrambled home an effort.

Then, just twelve minutes later, Sterling struck to give City the lead.

Spurs were still going through on away goals, but City were now rampant. Son couldn't see how Spurs were going to hold on.

City got their inevitable fourth goal from Sergio Agüero in the second half. Now *they* were going through.

"I can barely keep track of all of this," Son murmured to himself. All he knew was that another Spurs goal would make it 4-3, and Spurs would then go through on the away goal.

Minutes later, they got that goal.

Fernando Llorente, on as a sub, bundled home from a corner. There were appeals for handball from the City defenders, but with VAR in use the ref waved away the appeals and gave the goal.

Then, in the 93rd minute, disaster struck. Sergio Agüero burst into the box and cut the ball back to Raheem Sterling, who slammed it past Lloris.

Now City were going through.

Son sunk to his knees. Once more, the chance of a trophy had been snatched from him.

Then Son suddenly noticed that the ref had his finger to his ear – they were checking VAR on the goal.

It turned out that Agüero was offside in the build-up and the goal was disallowed!

Then, a few minutes later, the ref blew the final whistle.

Son didn't know what to do or where to go. Against all the odds they had knocked City out of the Champions League. Spurs were into the Champions League semi-finals!

"If we can win like this, then there's no reason we can't win the whole thing!" Dele Alli shouted, as they came off the pitch.

"You're absolutely right," an ecstatic Son replied.

25
WHO'S IT GOING TO BE?

November 2019, Tottenham Hotspur training ground,
London, England

"Who do you think it's going to be?" Harry Kane asked, as they sat together in the canteen.

"I don't know," Son shrugged. "I don't see anybody who can live up to Poch."

The win against Man City had started an incredible run in the Champions League. Spurs had battled past Ajax in dramatic fashion and ended up in the final against Liverpool. That had been a tough game with Liverpool beating them comfortably 2-0.

It was still only November, but already the Premier League was out of Spurs' reach, they were out of the League Cup and, after the way they'd been thrashed 7-2 at home by Bayern Munich, any chance of winning the Champions League was also completely gone.

It was the final straw for the Spurs board and Mauricio Pochettino had been sacked.

Nobody knew who was going to replace him – and the players were, unsurprisingly, nervous.

"I heard it's Mourinho," Harry Winks said quietly.

"No way," Kane said. "They wouldn't appoint Mourinho – he's way too defensive and negative. He wouldn't suit us at all."

"He always gets trophies, though," Son said, thinking about the number of trophies he'd seen Mourinho lifting over the years.

"Yeah, but he upsets everyone," Harry Winks added. "Do you really want a trophy under a guy like that?"

"Yeah, I think I would," Son replied. His desperation for a trophy was all he cared about now.

26
THE NEW GUY

November 2019, Tottenham Hotspur training ground,
London, England

They didn't have to wait long before the new manager was announced. Just as Harry Winks had predicted, it was José Mourinho.

He arrived to much fanfare and excitement. Mourinho had a different aura about him from Pochettino. This was a man who had won trophies everywhere he'd been, and he carried himself with a particular attitude.

This was a man who was going to win at all costs.

On his arrival, Mourinho summoned each player in turn into his office, to discuss with each of them individually his plans for the upcoming season.

Before long, it was Son's turn to go into his office.

José obviously hadn't been there that long, so things were still a bit of a mess, but Son could already see the little José touches – the photo of him being hoisted up by his Inter players after knocking Barcelona out of the Champions League, José himself holding the Champions League trophy after winning it with Porto in 2004 ...

"You like being called Sonny?" José said, sticking out a hand as Son entered.

"Yeah, that's good," he said, shaking the man's hand. If Son had told his 14-year-old self that one day he'd be face-to-face with José Mourinho, he'd never have believed it.

"I know we're a little off the pace this season," José continued, "but I think we can pull it back, get top four and get into the Champions League."

"Yeah – I mean that's definitely what I want," Son agreed.

"I also want to make a big push for the FA Cup," José said. "It's important to get that first trophy under our belt, it sets the tone."

"I agree," Son nodded.

"Look, Sonny," Jose said. "You're a nice guy, and you're a great player. But nice guys, they don't win anything in football. You need an edge, a desire to go one step further and to do whatever it takes to win. Have you got that? Are you prepared to take that step?"

"I want a trophy," Son said simply. "That's all I want right now."

"You stick with me and I'll get you a trophy," José said. "I'll get everyone in this team a medal around their necks. It might not be this year, but if by the end of next year you haven't got a medal hanging round your neck, then I'll let you go for free to whoever you want to join."

"Really?" Son asked, a little confused.

"I *guarantee* you will win a trophy with me, Sonny," José said. "As long as you're willing to do everything I ask of you on that pitch."

27

HIS GREATEST GOAL

December 2019, Tottenham Hotspur Stadium, London, England
Spurs v Burnley

José's reign started well, with consecutive wins over West Ham and Bournemouth. But after a midweek defeat to Man United, there were already questions about whether he was the right choice for the club.

Today's game, just a few days after losing to Man U, was at home against Burnley.

"You're my main man today, Sonny," José said in the

dressing room. "So go out there and dominate this game."

The match started well, with both Harry Kane and Lucas Moura scoring inside the first 10 minutes.

Spurs were cruising, but Son wasn't happy. He hadn't scored yet, and he wanted to prove to José that he was indeed the main man at Spurs.

Twenty minutes later, Son got the ball deep in his own half. He started running forward with it, shrugging off the challenge of a Burnley midfielder.

Quickly he was over the half-way line, still going. He was surrounded by a number of Burnley players, but he couldn't see any of his team-mates.

He kept going, gliding past Matthew Lowton and Erik Pieters and skipping past another clumsy challenge. He was now thirty yards from goal, dodging yet another challenge.

Then suddenly he was in the box and, as the keeper came out, he calmly slotted it past him.

GOAL!

Without a doubt, it was the best goal of Son's career, the best he'd ever scored.

"That was like Messi or Maradona, or someone!" Harry Kane shouted, chasing after him.

"I thought you'd be annoyed I didn't square it for you!" Son laughed. "I tried to pass to Dele too, but I couldn't find him. So I just kept going."

Spurs added two more goals to run out 5-0 winners. It was a huge victory, sending a message to the rest of the Premier League and hopefully setting the tone for the new José Mourinho era.

Son was at the centre of José's plans for that new era and, for him, it couldn't come quickly enough.

28

BACK - AND ON FORM

August 2021, Tottenham Hotspur Stadium, London, England
Spurs v Man City

"Nice to have the fans back, eh Sonny?" said Dele, as they stood on the pitch, waiting for the ref to start the first Spurs game of the new Premier League season.

The previous season had been badly interrupted by the COVID pandemic, and what matches were played had taken place in empty stadiums. It just hadn't been the same without the fans.

Now it felt great to be getting back to normal.

But in the last year so much had changed for Son at Spurs. Mourinho had left, his reign not being anywhere near the success that he had promised – or that Son had hoped for.

Now they had a new manager, Nuno Espírito Santo, and no one really knew what to expect.

There was no Harry Kane for today's game against Man City either. He was trying to leave Spurs and was sitting this game out.

Son knew that, in Kane's absence, this was the opportunity for him to step up.

Man City started the game quickly, creating a few chances in the first 15 minutes, but Spurs managed to settle down and started to control the tempo a little more.

At half-time there was still no score, and Nuno was pleased.

"Well done, lads," he said to the players in the dressing room. "We're shutting them out well, and they're struggling to create chances. Now let's hit them on the counter and snatch a win."

The second half started with City controlling lots of the ball again, but when Spurs won it back they countered fast.

It wasn't long before they were able to take advantage.

Ten minutes after the break, Son received the ball out on the right wing, but without Kane there was no one in the box ready for a cross.

So instead he stepped inside onto his left foot and unleashed a shot from just outside the box. The ball snaked past City keeper Ederson and hit the back of the net.

GOAL!

Son had put Spurs into the lead!

The stadium erupted as the newly returned Spurs fans savoured the goal. Son felt exhilarated by the crowd's enthusiasm. It was amazing – he'd missed the fans more than he realised.

With no more goals in the game, Spurs held out for the full three points, in what was a huge win against the Premier League favourites.

"I think you might be right, Sonny," Lucas Moura

said as they left the pitch. "I think this might be the year we win it."

Son nodded. All his years of working hard back home in South Korea, in Germany and now in the Premier League, perhaps they had all led to this.

He wasn't just playing in this team, he was one of its stars – and he knew that they depended totally on his skill and his experience.

He knew that whatever happened he was going to go down as a Spurs legend and one of South Korea's best ever players.

All he needed to do now was get a medal around his neck and a trophy in his hands.

He knew he was close.

Perhaps he *was* right. Perhaps this might be the year he did it.

HOW MANY
HAVE YOU READ?